Marisol

Marisol

Curated by Judy Collischan

Organized by Lucinda H. Gedeon

Essay by Eleanor Heartney

Neuberger Museum of Art

Purchase College,

State University of New York

Published in conjunction with the exhibition

Marisol

Neuberger Museum of Art,
Purchase College, State University of New York
Purchase, New York
June 17 – September 2, 2001

Delaware Art Museum
November 19, 2001 – January 29, 2002

Exhibition and Publication made possible with funds from the Friends
of the Neuberger Museum of Art, The Richard Florsheim Art Fund,
New York State Council on the Arts, and the Westchester Arts
Council with funds from the County of Westchester.

General Editor: Lucinda H. Gedeon

Design: Marc Zaref Design, Inc.

Printing: The Studley Press

Photography: Courtesy © Marisol and Marlborough Gallery,
pgs. 8, 10, 16, 18-22, 33-47, 49-52; Courtesy Marisol, pgs. 56, 59, 63, 64;
Allan Finkelman, pgs. 21, 42; Jim Frank, pgs. 15, 26-32, 53; Michael
Kleinberg, pg. 48; Bill McLemore, pg. 37; O.E. Nelson, pg. 40; Malcolm
Varon, cover, pgs. 20, 41, 43

Library of Congress Control Number: 2001117615

ISBN: 0 934032-17-3

Cover: (detail) *John, Washington and Emily Roebling Crossing the Brooklyn
Bridge for the First Time*, 1989, wood, plaster, stain, 104 x 78 x 48 inches.
Courtesy Marlborough Gallery, New York

Contents

Foreword and Acknowledgments

At twenty years of age, a well-traveled and well-educated Marisol Escobar moved to New York in 1950. As a child she knew she was an artist and pursued her creative talents throughout her teen-age years in Los Angeles and in Paris at the École des Beaux Arts. In New York she studied at the Arts Student League, The New School for Social Research and with Hans Hofmann. Within the decade Marisol, by which she prefers to be known, had been accorded her first solo exhibition at the Leo Castelli Gallery, participated in a number of group exhibitions here and abroad, and was becoming well-recognized as a talented sculptor with a signature style. For the past forty years, this remarkable artist has created an extraordinary body of work that addresses themes related to the human condition, human foibles, relationships and social satire with tremendous wit and good humor.

Having long admired Marisol's work, and recognized its importance in 20th-century art, this exhibition was a distinct pleasure to coordinate. From the beginning it was a collaborative effort of many individuals. The entire staff is to be congratulated, but I want to particularly acknowledge former Associate Director for Curatorial Affairs Judy Collischan for her curatorial work on the initial selection of the pieces; Assistant Curator Jacqueline Shilkoff for coordinating the loan forms, photography requests and assisting with installation; Curatorial Assistant Michele Matusic for assisting with the chronology; Jose Smith for his work on installation; Museum Registrar Patricia Magnani, who coordinated all the shipping of the works and arranged for the exhibition to travel to the Delaware Art Museum; and Claire Powers who assisted with proofreading the text.

It was wonderful to work with art historian and critic Eleanor Heartney again, and I want to thank her for her catalogue essay, which places Marisol's work into the broader context of 20th-century Modernism. I am grateful to Jim Frank for his photographic work for the catalogue, and for the catalogue's design as well as for their work on the layout and design of the exhibition our gratitude goes to Cindy and Marc Zaref of Marc Zaref Design, Inc. I would also like to thank artist Larry Rivers for his help with the identification of the some of the individuals who appear in the photographs in the chronology.

I am also grateful to the many lenders to the exhibition, who graciously have shared their works so that we might present this exhibition for so many to enjoy. Our gratitude goes to: Guy and Nora Barron; the Albright-Knox Art Gallery,

Buffalo, New York; Elizabeth B. Blake; Colorado Springs Fine Arts Center, Colorado Springs, Colorado; Vera List; Marisol; The Marlborough Gallery, New York; The Museum of Modern Art, New York; Roy R. Neuberger; Monica and Rick Segal; and Janet and Joseph Shein. I am particularly grateful to Robert Buck, director of The Marlborough Gallery, New York, for all of his help in securing photographs of the works in the exhibition.

This exhibition would not have been possible without the financial assistance of the Friends of the Neuberger Museum of Art, the New York State Council on the Arts, the Westchester Arts Council with funds from Westchester County Government, and The Richard Florsheim Art Fund, to whom we are tremendously grateful.

In the end, it is Marisol and her exceptional work that we celebrate with this exhibition and its catalogue. We thank her for the opportunity to present this survey that represents more than four decades of her life's work as an artist. She was very giving of her time in the planning for the exhibition and in proofing material for the catalogue, for which I extend my heartfelt appreciation.

Lucinda H. Gedeon, Ph.D.
Director

Marisol with *Portrait of My Father,* 1985

8

Marisol: A Sculptor of Modern Life

by Eleanor Heartney

In 1863, the critic and poet Charles Baudelaire challenged the artists of his day to turn from tired academic subjects and allegorical motifs and take on the exciting subject of modernity. They should aim, he suggested, to become a "painter of modern life." Such an artist, he noted, would be one who "enters into the crowd as though it were an immense reservoir of electrical energy. Or we might liken him to a mirror as vast as the crowd itself; or to a kaleidoscope gifted with consciousness, responding to each one of its movements and reproducing the multiplicity of life and the flickering grace of all elements of life."[1]

For over a century, Baudelaire's exhortation has continued to resonate among artists. His advice seems particularly pertinent to the period of the early 1960s, at the moment when the inward turning Abstract Expressionist movement began to give way to the extroverted ebullience of Pop. Pop art took a variety of forms, and a number of very different artists were linked to the movement at one time or another. But in its "classic" phase, Pop was an art that celebrated the modernity of postwar-America and found inspiration in the symbols and symptoms of its new prosperity.

Today when we think of Pop art, the names that most immediately come to mind are those of Andy Warhol, Roy Lichtenstein, James Rosenquist, Jim Dine and Tom Wesselman. These artists explored the seductions of advertising and blandishments of commercial culture, using a style borrowed from the mass media. They focused on the way that images create desire, and they created art which expressed, not so much how people lived, as how they felt they should live.

This is in contrast to more traditional forms of social commentary. For this sort of exploration, we must turn to a different group of artists who were affiliated with Pop, but in retrospect, involved in something quite different. These artists focused on people and their relationships rather than on the things and media images that surrounded them. They revealed what was going on behind the American dream—the fate of those untouched by postwar prosperity, the loneliness engendered by an atomized society, the emptiness of material success. Of course in the 1960s, media was also part of the story they told. So they also touch on the cult of celebrity, the striving for status, and the dream of wealth and sex appeal. But these weren't the whole story.

The artists I have in mind invited audiences to consider a much broader tapestry of American life than that provided by the media machine. They include Red Grooms, who exhibited a rollicking good humor that gave a carnival quality to his depiction of the diversity of urban life; Edward Kienholz, who presented a dark vision of the hidden horrors of a paternalistic, conformist society; George Segal, who focused on the dignity of anonymous citizens; finally, it included Marisol, who recreated both the mask and the human story that lay behind it.

Of these artists, Marisol is perhaps the least understood, in part because the wide range of her themes and subjects does not allow for easy categorization. Additionally, her association with Pop encouraged a surface reading that ran counter to the layered subtleties embedded in her work. With the passage of time, it is now possible to see her work more clearly, to disentangle it from a superficial reading of Pop, and to trace out the various threads which tie it all together.

On one hand there are wickedly satirical works like *The Family,* 1962 (plate 9), which takes on the social games of the status seekers of 60s America. But there are also deeply empathetic works, i.e. *Cuban Children with Goat* (plate 20), which bring us an uncondescending view of the world shaped by privation and poverty. She is an artist capable of creating both a wonderful parody of the macho ideal represented by John Wayne (plate 12) and a reverent homage to South African Bishop Desmond Tutu (plate 17). She has made deeply personal works like *Mi Mama Y Yo* (plate 13), a poignant portrait of herself as a little girl with her mother, who died when she was eleven; witty, caustic representations of world leaders like Franco, De Gaulle, John F. Kennedy and Lyndon Johnson and sensitive depictions of artists like Picasso (fig. 1), de Kooning (plate 16) and Georgia O'Keeffe (plate 15) in the later years of their lives.

Commentators are often more comfortable with artists whom they can easily box, but Marisol defies such expectations. Nevertheless, there is a thread that ties her work together. It is, as Baudelaire suggested, an ability to engage sympathetically with the world around her.

This was stimulated, no doubt, by the peripatetic nature of her early life. Born in Paris in 1930 to Venezuelan parents, Marisol spent her first years traveling in Europe with her family, and then commuting between Caracas and

figure 1 **Picasso**, 1977, wood and plaster,
134 ¹/₂ x 73 ¹/₂ x 73 ¹/₂ inches. Private Collection

the United States and Europe. After her mother's death in 1941, she went to boarding school. Her father continued to travel between Caracas, New York, Europe and also Los Angeles, where Marisol attended high school. When it came time for higher education, she declared her interest in art and announced that she wished to study in Paris. Though her father supported her interest in art, he felt that she would be safer in New York. Marisol tells this story with a wry amusement, because of course, as it turns out in the early fifties New York was the center of a bohemian art culture whose excesses have since become legendary.

For an aspiring young artist, it was an exciting moment to enter the New York art world. She took classes at the Art Students League, the New School of Social Research and Hans Hofmann's painting school. At this time she still considered herself as a painter. This began to change as she came into contact with sculptors like William King, a creator of witty, pseudo primitive figures, and with the tradition of American folk art and pre-Columbian art on which she drew. Her earliest exhibited work consisted of tiny clay figurines set like relics or specimens in the compartments of an old printer's type box. She began to expand her repertoire, creating figures from wood and bronze as well. *Queen*, 1957 (plate 1), is an excellent example of this early work. A terra cotta crown of tiny figure-like fingers rests atop the head of a carved wood bust of a woman, suggesting Marisol's interest in folk art and "primitive" sculpture. By the end of the decade, she was receiving favorable press in major art magazines.

An important turning point occurred in 1960, when she came upon a potato sack full of hat forms while visiting friends in Easthampton, New York. These became the basis for the first works that are recognizably Marisol. The hat forms became full-scale human heads and were set in compartments or atop simple painted blocks. This exhibition contains one of these early works. *Tea for Three*, 1960 (plate 6), consists of three hat-form heads on top of a block painted with vertical red, yellow and blue stripes. The heads are clown-like with white plaster casts of parts of the artist's own face, giving them fragmentary references to realism. One is topped with a hat in the shape of a building. It is possible to see references here to some of the other artists who were also coming to the forefront of the avant garde art world. The casts suggest Jasper Johns' 1955 *Target with Plaster Casts*, in which a large encaustic painting of a target is topped by a row of small compartments containing cast fragments of his own body although Marisol had not seen his work at this point. The building/hat, meanwhile, brings to mind a 1959 performance by Red Grooms entitled *The Burning Building*, whose set consisted of a careening cardboard cityscape that presaged his later environmental works.

But whether such similar elements were direct influences or simply part of the period's general air of experimentation, it is clear that Marisol has already begun staking out her own unique territory. The stiff bodies with expressive faces, the ingenious use of found and created elements, the interest in character and the deadpan wit all are already evident in this early work.

Mariol's career received an important boost when she was included in the groundbreaking 1961 *The Art of Assemblage* exhibition at the Museum of Modern Art. This exhibition picked up on an aesthetic that was becoming widespread both in Europe and the United States. The term "assemblage" itself, which refers to art that incorporates real objects, was first used in 1955 by Jean Dubuffet to distinguish his own work from the more three dimensional collages of Picasso and Braque. The sprawling exhibition included such early twentieth-century pioneers as Marcel Duchamp, Pablo Picasso, Kurt Schwhitters, Max Ernst and Andre Breton, as well as more recent artists like Louise Nevelson, Joseph Cornell, Jean Tinguely, and Arman. Among the youngest artists were Robert Rauschenberg, Jasper Johns, Edward Kienholz, H.C. Westerman, Robert Indiana, Lucas Samaras, and, of course, Marisol.

Marisol's contribution was a sculpture entitled *From France* (plate 5), an amusing portrayal of a couple of tourists. In this work, two cylindrical hat-form heads with berets top a rough block of wood. One of the man's legs ends in a real baby shoe and their joint fronts contain plaster casts over a packing sign with the stenciled words "FROM FRANCE." Like *Tea for Three* (plate 6), this work celebrated Marisol's enjoyment of scavenging. As she told interviewer Avis Berman in 1984, "All my early work came from the street. It was magical for me to find things. There was a thrown-out baby carriage, so I made a mother with her baby in the carriage. I looked down at an old beam in the gutter and saw the Mona Lisa. When I drew in the face and sanded it, the grain of the wood made a smile by itself… So many things like that happened to me."[2]

The Art of Assemblage made the case for the diversity and the importance of assemblage to twentieth-century artists. It also set the stage for the emergence, a few years later, of a movement that came to be known as Pop. While Pop later crystallized in the public mind as a movement that centered around artists like Andy Warhol and Roy Lichtenstein, and parodied advertising and pop culture, in its more amorphous beginning Pop was also known as Neo-Dada. This title, with its reference to the sometimes-bitter social commentary of artists like Max Ernst, Francis Picabia and Man Ray, carries darker connotations and connects to the thread of social critique which runs through much of Marisol's work.

As an erstwhile Pop artist, Marisol was also associated in the public mind with Andy Warhol, and indeed, he memorably dubbed her "The first girl artist with glamour."[3] But, as an artist who arrived in New York at the moment when the last golden glow of Abstract Expressionism overlapped with the birth of Pop, she also remained drawn to the psychological intensity of artists like de Kooning and Franz Kline, whom she met during forays to the Cedar Bar.

Certainly, some of the sculptures Marisol created during this time conformed to the upbeat ethos of Pop. For instance, *The Bathers*, 1961-62 (plate 8), is a lighthearted work which depicts three women in bathing suits lolling casually in the sun. The work reveals Marisol's increasingly sophisticated use of three dimensions. One woman's head and torso are painted on a backdrop, while her carved legs extend out into the air. The other two figures are fully dimensional, but their bodies shift between smoothly shaped wood that evokes their womanly curves and sections that retain the blocky quality of the wood from which they have been created. As an ensemble, the group is suffused with an easygoing eroticism—and in fact the woman in the foreground lies on her stomach exposing a pair of satiny white buttocks cast from plaster.

But if *The Bathers* shares the hedonism and cheeky sensuality of work by Pop masters like Warhol, Rosenquist and Wesselman, Marisol was also capable of work that was sobering and serious. *The Family* (plate 9) is based on a vintage photograph of a rural Southern family in the 1920s and 30s that she rescued from the trash bin of her studio mate, a photographer who reproduced family photographs for a living. The work is completely frontal, depicting a fatherless family posing stiffly in their modest Sunday best for a professional photographer. As in *The Bathers*, parts of the figures and faces are painted on a flat backdrop, while others protrude into space. Particularly striking is the fully carved face of the baby who sits quietly in his mother's lap. Behind the group an elaborate ironwork pattern from the original photograph is painted over a pair of doors Marisol found on the street outside her studio. In contrast to her more satirical depictions of members of the middle and leisure class, Marisol endows this group with a sense of strength and dignity that is utterly without irony.

In the giddy atmosphere of the early sixties, Marisol's intentions were sometimes misconstrued. For instance, in 1963 she was commissioned by *Life Magazine* to create a work that would appear in an issue on the movies. Marisol decided to depict the cinematic icon John Wayne. Using a toy horse from Mexico as the model for his steed, she presented Wayne as a cross between a merry-go-round figure and a weathervane (plate 12). The red horse's legs fly out in front and back while the cowboy figure sits stiffly in the saddle. Suggesting his quick draw, he has an extra hand, so that we see the same hand resting the gun by his side and raised in front of his chest. The work, which appeared the same year as Warhol's Marilyns, was seen in a similar light, as a work of adulation to a glamorous movie star. But in fact, Marisol confesses that she always disliked John Wayne, and believed that he couldn't act. Viewed in this light, it becomes clear that this work actually serves as a satirical riff on the super-macho image that Wayne embodied.

By the time this work appeared in *Life Magazine*, Marisol had become a major figure in contemporary American art. She was known inside and outside the art world, was prominently included in such important surveys of the scene as the Museum of Modern Art's 1963 exhibition *The Americans* as well as Annuals, museum exhibitions presenting the year's highlights, in New York, Chicago, and Pittsburgh. She was the subject of numerous newspaper and magazine profiles, many of which focuses more on her exotic good looks and reputedly glamorous lifestyle than on a serious evaluation of her work.

But even in the glare of the public eye, Marisol managed, as the sixties progressed, to continue her formal and thematic explorations. Much of her work focused on explicit social commentary, in which she tended to satirize the prosperous, while conveying sympathy for the less fortunate. The range is surprisingly wide. There is the playful insouciance of *Women Sitting on a Mirror*, 1965-66 (fig. 2), in which the women's figures, elongated by the reflection of the mirror on which they rest, are topped by saucy hats, which are actually forms that Marisol found in a plastic store near her neighborhood. One, in particular, has a broad brim reminiscent of the hat worn by Audrey Hepburn in *Breakfast at Tiffany's*, a popular film at the time.

This satirical dig at women of fashion could not be further from the spirit of *Mi Mama y Yo*, 1968 (plate 13), a rare autobiographical work in steel and aluminum which the artist created for an outdoor setting. This poignant work presents Marisol as a young girl standing on a bench and holding a perforated parasol over her mother, who died when she was eleven. The two bodies are created from similar pink minimalist forms, conveying a sense of their psychic connection. Heads, hands and feet are cast in a realistic manner, reflecting the details evident in the family photograph on which this work is based. Again, there is no irony here, just a sense of the comfortable bond between mother and child.

A completely different take on childhood appears in a pair of works from 1962 and 63. *Baby Boy* and *Baby Girl* (plates 10 and 11) are horrific visions of giant children who grasp miniature Marisol dolls. *Baby Girl* measures six feet and *Baby Boy* measures seven. They sit or stand stiffly in their best clothes, exuding an almost monstrous complacency that seems to suggest the unreflective self-absorption of postwar-American culture.

By the end of the decade, Marisol felt a need to take a break from the frenzied pace of the New York art world.

She spent a year traveling in Asia, becoming acquainted with Asian art and learning scuba diving and underwater photography. When she returned to New York in 1970, she found herself in an entirely new frame of mind. She began a series of fish sculptures. Carved in smoothly polished wood with plaster masks cast from her own face, they have, as she concedes, a weapon-like quality, suggesting missiles or rockets. Yet there is also something both elegant and alien about these works that suggested a change of direction. *Fishman,* 1973 (plate 14), for instance, is an enigmatic, dreamlike sculpture. It consists of a polished male body stepping slightly forward in a pose reminiscent of Greek *Kouros* figures. He has a fish head and holds a whole fish in one arm. At his feet, like an animal fetish, is a toucan with Marisol's face.

Reflecting on this period, Marisol told an interviewer in 1975, "When I came back (from the far east) I felt like doing something very pure, just for the sake of it... I wanted to do something beautiful."[4] Marisol's critics were baffled, wondering where the witty satirist of the sixties has gone. But while this period of introspection did not last long, she emerged from it with a more mature set of concerns.

Recent decades have brought Marisol a number of new themes. She created a set of portraits of older artists, and began to work from specific historical events. She created a monumental sculptural reconstruction of da Vinci's *Last Supper* (fig. 3), as well as his *Virgin, Child, St. Anne and St. John* (fig. 4). But she also returned to earlier themes, continuing to examine the nature of family and social class.

The artist portraits, in particular, are the work of a mature artist reflecting on the meaning and demands of her vocation. In this series she celebrates artists whom she particularly admires. She has chosen to represent them later in life, emphasizing the lined faces and careworn expressions that have developed during decades of creative struggle. "After

figure 3 **Self Portrait Looking at the Last Supper**, 1981-84, wood, plywood, charcoal, paint, brownstone, plaster, aluminum, 121 × 358 × 67 inches. Collection The Metropolitan Museum of Art, New York; gift of Mr. and Mrs. Roberto C. Polo, 1986

figure 4 **Madonna, Child, St. Anne and St. John**, 1978,
charcoal on wood, plaster, tone, 144 x 196 x 61 inches.
Collection, El Museo de Arte Contemporáneo, Caracas, Venezuela

fifty" George Orwell remarked, "everyone has the face he
deserves."[5] In these works, Marisol gives a remarkable repre-
sentation of the real meaning of "character."

Her *Portrait of Georgia O'Keeffe With Dogs*, 1977
(plate 15) is based on photographs she took during a visit to
O'Keeffe in New Mexico. The 90-year old artist sits bolt
upright on a stump, her walking cane in hand. She is flanked
by her two pet show dogs, which stand by her like guardians.
The most remarkable aspects of this sculpture are the deeply
wrinkled hands, familiar to us from Alfred Stieglitz's photographs of O'Keeffe, and the magnificent furrowed face. She
has a regal bearing that commands immediate respect.

Marisol's *Portrait of de Kooning* (plate 16) meanwhile,
is more casual. An old friend from her days at the Cedar Bar,
he sits in a sturdy copy of his favorite rocking chair, with three

hands, in what may be a comment on his painting skill. Again, the head is what draws us, as its roughly carved surfaces
evoke an artist deeply immersed in his own thoughts. "de Kooning was my hero—actually he still is my hero," Marisol told
interviewer Avis Berman, "and I learned a lot from him."[6]

Marisol also did portraits of artists including Louise Nevelson, Pablo Picasso, Martha Graham, Marcel Duchamp,
William Burroughs and Virgil Thompson. The only artist in this series whom she never met was Picasso, yet he clearly looms
large as an artistic father figure. For his portrait she combined two famous photographs of him (fig. 1). In one he was sitting
on the beach, and she has faithfully reproduced his bare legs and gnarled feet coming out of a rough block of wood. The
other photograph showed him seated on a chair in his studio. Marisol has copied this chair and given Picasso two sets of
hands, one resting on the chair arms, the other on his knees. His enormous aquiline nose protrudes from a grooved face
with deep-set troubled eyes. All the artists in this series are seated, because, as Marisol has remarked, she felt she needed
to give them a place to rest at their advanced age.[7]

These artist portraits are not the only ones that convey admirations. Marisol also began to turn to history and to politics for heroic figures. While earlier portraits of political leaders like de Gaulle, Queen Elizabeth and Lyndon Johnson were often saturated with playful satire, there is nothing but admiration in her sculpture of *Bishop Desmond Tutu*, 1988 (plate 17). A world-renowned spokesperson for the disenfranchised of apartheid era South Africa, Tutu is present in Marisol's work as a massive, implacable force for righteousness. She has set a realistically carved head on a massive purple box with a lighted cutaway in the form of a cross. Protruding from the box is a single hand that holds his bishop's staff. The whole work resonates with a sense of moral resolve.

Blackfoot Delegation to Washington 1916 (fig. 5) created in 1993, deals with a similarly appalling historical moment. This work, which came about when a group of Native Americans invited artists to participate in the American Pavilion at the World's Fair in Seville by submitting an artwork in exchange for a shaman blessing. Marisol was the only artist who responded to their invitation. This exchange inspired the sculpture, which is based on an old photograph of a famous meeting in which the Blackfoot Indians attempted to negotiate a land settlement with the US Government. The five delegates face the viewer with somber resolution. The three figures in the foreground wear native garb and carry accoutrements of their vanishing lifestyle. Standing stiffly behind them are two darker figures who have conceded to the conventions of their conquerors by donning suits and ties. There is nothing patronizing in Marisol's depiction, no reference to the stereotypical cigar store Indian or the comic Redskin of the Wild West Show. Instead, she presents her delegates as grave and tragic figures locked in an unsuccessful battle with the forces of history.

A happier moment in American history is chronicled in *John, Washington and Emily Roebling Crossing the Brooklyn Bridge for the First Time* 1989 (plate 19). This

figure 5 **Blackfoot Delegation to Washington, 1916**, 1993, wood, mixed media, 80 x 60 x 42 inches. Collection Palmer Museum of Art, The Pennsylvania State University, University Park, PA

work, which was commissioned for a public memorial that was never built, evokes the first carriage ride over the Brooklyn Bridge by the triumvirate of family members responsible for its construction. In the center is the patriarch, John Roebling, who designed the bridge. He thrusts out his arm in a gesture that speaks both of resolution and leadership. Next to him stands his son, Washington, who continued to work on the bridge after his father's death. But the real hero of the piece seems to be Emily, Washington's wife, who dominates the tableau in her sweeping red dress. She completed the bridge after her husband became disabled, and she holds the rooster, which she is said to have carried as a symbol of victory on this first auspicious crossing. Clearly feeling a sense of identification with the vision and the grit required to see such an undertaking through, Marisol told interviewer Paul Gardner in 1989 that, "The Roeblings symbolized courage and strength, which produced a work of art."[8]

These new themes have appeared alongside older ones in Marisol's more recent work. The family unit, which she has both satirized and celebrated over the years, receives a more overtly political twist in the 1987 tableau *Poor Family I* (fig. 6). This work, and several related ones, followed Marisol's participation in an exhibition organized to bring attention to the problems of world hunger and over population. In a statement for that show, Marisol wrote, "In some parts of the world people are on diets, obese from overeating, while in other parts, people are starving to death. I would like to see a more balanced way of sharing food and life."[9]

Poor Family I dramatizes that problem. It represents a large Latin American family with mother, father, ten children and two dogs. They crowd together, older children holding younger ones, almost obscuring the corner of a small table covered with a red and white checked tablecloth. The likelihood of its ever holding enough food to satisfy all of them seems slim. Meanwhile, they are separated from us by a low pile of stone rubble, which only seems to reinforce a sense of their privation.

Marisol revisits similar territory in her 1995 *Cuban Children with Goat* (plate 20). Here we see a raggedy dressed group of children sitting on a weathered beam pulling at a reluctant goat which, one presumes, they are taking to market to sell. They regard us with grimacing expressions, which, Marisol reports, is exactly how the group of children on whom this work is based posed for the camera when she took their picture during a trip to Cuba in the mid-nineties.

Not all Marisol's more recent works are so serious. *The Airplane,* 1983 (fig. 7), is based on a real life acquaintance—the grandfather of a friend who owned a ranch in Venezuela. Though already a very old man when she met him, this patriarch used a small plane to get to and from his ranch. Marisol loved the idea of making a sculpture that put together a man from an earlier era with a means of transport associated with our own. She depicts him as he appeared in a photograph she saw, gingerly holding out his cane in front of an airplane that is a scaled-down replica of the one he actually used.

The collapse of time frames is also one aspect of *The Last Supper,* a monumental sculptural recreation of Leonardo da Vinci's masterpiece (fig. 3). Christ is carved from a salvaged brownstone, while the rest of the figures are created from pieces of wood. Though the subject is ostensibly religious, Marisol insists that was not her intention in creating this piece. In a 1989 interview, she explained, "Leonardo's masterpiece is really about the Renaissance, not religion. His setting is an aristocratic dinner in Italy. I think he used models from the street and arranged their robes after the fashion of the day …

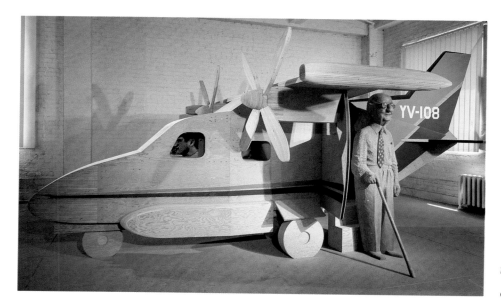

figure 7 **The Airplane**, 1983, wood and paint, 144 x 196 x 61 inches. Collection El Museo de Arte Contemporáneo, Caracas, Venezuela

I suppose if someone were to do the Last Supper today, it would take place in a restaurant like the Odeon."[10]

She has placed a sculpture of herself in front of the tableau, noting, "Because I studied it so much, I put my portrait there."[11] This work marks a return to the self-portrait motif, which had largely disappeared from her work after the *Fish* series. It seems here to represent an identification with the audience, which is looking at her work.

The most recent works in this exhibition are from her series of *Magritte* (plates 25-29). In these works, Marisol's old playfulness is in full evidence. The surrealist artist is represented in a set of stiff comic figures in bowler hats and real umbrellas. The work could be seen as a mediation on the practice of illusion, which makes art possible. It doesn't seem farfetched to imagine that Marisol feels a certain kinship with Magritte, another master of absurdist displacement and sly critic of the pomposities of the middle class. The multiple Magrittes here seem ready to take flight on the wings of their outstretched umbrellas, unlikely avatars of the artistic imagination.

For over four decades, Marisol has been engaged in weaving a marvelous tapestry of human foibles, tragedies and ambitions. From this end of her career, her distance from the conventional notion of Pop Art is increasingly clear. Yet there is no other movement which seems capable of encompassing the range of her achievements. As I suggested at the outset, she seems best placed with other social commentators like Ed Kienholz, Red Grooms, and George Segal. On a formal level, she is perhaps closest to Kienholz, who also created figures and human environments out of the detritus of

modern urban life. But her tone is very different than his. Kienholz tends toward horrific portraits of the family and the American scene. His figures are composed of found objects—sewing tables, tricycles and baby strollers, fish bowls, animal bones—arranged to bring out a sense of dehumanization and degradation.

Compare this with Marisol's family portraits. She was capable of highly satirical depictions—for instance, a 1963 *The Family* (fig. 8), which depicts an upscale middle class family with a distant, stalwart dad, a mindless fashionable mom and four children, two insufferable toddlers and two babies in a carriage. But she also can deal with the subject with great empathy, as we have seen in works like the 1962 *The Family*

figure 8 **The Family**, 1963, mixed media.
The Robert B. Mayer Family Collection

(plate 8) and *Poor Family I* (fig. 6). For Kienholz, the family is a nightmare, while for Marisol, it is the building block of society and subject to the same tensions and difficulties as the rest of the culture. She gives form to Baudelaire's remark, "The lover of life makes the whole world his family."[12]

Another social commentator, Red Grooms, shares her cheekiness and astute observation of telling details, but he is also more completely a parodist. Like Marisol, Grooms has created numerous portraits of other artists, but these tend to focus on the absurdity of the avant gardist impulse as it appears to the non-art public. And when he deals with Native Americans, he tends to draw his references from immediately recognizable media images rather than direct experience.

Oddly, considering how different their work is formally, the artist whose vision comes closest to Marisol's is George Segal. His white plaster casts of anonymous urban types in generic urban settings share the sense of humanism and sympathy that has been increasingly apparent in Marisol's more recent work. Like her, he is drawn to the vulnerabilities and the poignant struggles of his characters. He reminds us that we are all part of the same crazy world.

In the end, labels like Pop or Abstract Expressionism are less important than the enduring qualities of the art they describe. In Marisol's case what endures is the universality of the impulses she captures. Truly a sculptor of modern life, she evokes the venality of social climbers, the integrity of great artists, the contradictions of the powerful and the quiet dignity of dispossessed. She feels both their absurdity and their pain and encourages us to do the same.

1. Charles Baudelaire, "The Painter of Modern Life," reprinted in *The Painter of Modern Life and Other Essays*, trans. and ed. by Jonathan Mayne. (New York: Da Capo Press, 1964):12

2. Avis Berman, "A Bold and Incisive Way of Portraying Movers and Shakers," *Smithsonian 14* (Feb 1984): 56

3. Andy Warhol and Pat Hackett, *POPism: The Warhol 60s* (New York: Harcourt Brace Javanovich, 1980): 35

4. Quoted in Cindy Nemser, *ArtTalk*, (New York: Charles Scribner, 1975):190

5. George Orwell, "Extracts from a Manuscript Note-book," reprinted in *The Collected Essays, Journalism and Letters of George Orwell*. Ed. Sonia Orwell and Ian Angus (New York: Harcourt Brace Jovanovich, 1968): 515

6. Berman, "A Bold and Incisive way of Portraying Movers and Shakers," p. 57

7. Interview with the artist, September 2000

8. Paul Gardner, "Who is Marisol?" *ARTnews 88* (May 1989): 148

9. Artist statement for "International Art show for the End of World Hunger," traveling exhibition, 1987

10. Gardner, "Who is Marisol?" p. 149

11. Ibid

12. Baudelaire, "The Painter of Modern Life," p. 13

Plates

Queen 1957
wood and terra cotta, 29 3/4 x 13 1/2 x 9 inches
Collection Roy R. Neuberger

4 **My Wedding Cake** 1959
bronze, 20 x 11 x 9 inches
Collection of the artist

5 **From France** 1960
wood construction beam, painted and stenciled wood, carved wood,
found objects, plaster casts, 54 3/8 × 21 1/4 × 16 inches
Collection Elizabeth B. Blake

6 **Tea for Three** 1960
wood, acrylic paint and china, 64 × 22 × 27 inches
Collection of the artist

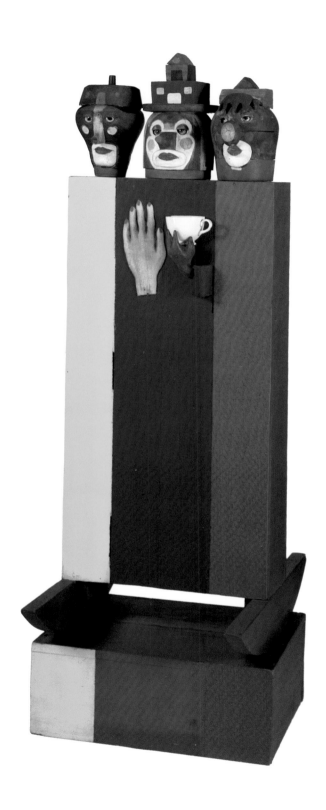

7 **The Blacks** 1962
wood, plaster, 84 × 12 × 6 inches
Private Collection

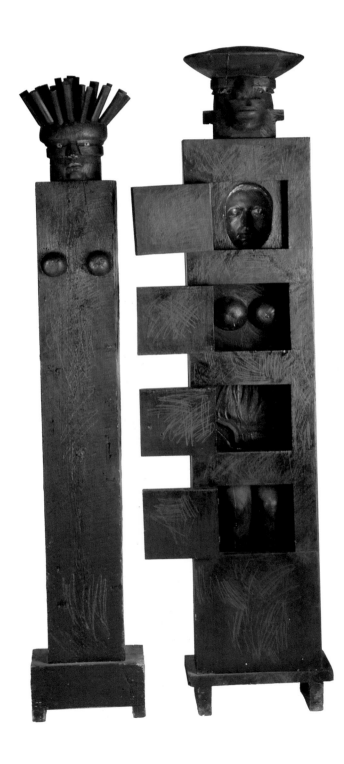

8 The Bathers 1961-62
wood and mixed media, 83 ⁷/₈ × 70 × 58 inches
Courtesy Marlborough Gallery, New York

painted wood and mixed media [three sections], 82 5/8 × 65 1/2 × 15 1/2 inches
Collection of The Museum of Modern Art, New York, New York
Advisory Committee Fund, 1962

10 Baby Boy 1962-63
painted wood and mixed media, 88 x 33 x 23 inches
Collection Vera List

11 Baby Girl 1963
wood and mixed media, 74 x 35 x 47 inches
Collection Albright-Knox Art Gallery, Buffalo, New York
Gift of Seymour H. Knox, 1964

12 **John Wayne** 1963
wood, pencil, oil, paint, plaster, steel
104 × 96 × 15 inches [113 inches high installed]
Collection Colorado Springs Fine Arts Center, Julianne Kemper
Gilliam Purchase Fund and Debutante Ball Purchase Fund

13 **Mi Mama Y Yo** 1968
steel and aluminum, 73 × 56 × 56 inches
Collection of the artist

14 **Fishman** 1973
wood and plaster, 50 × 22 × 30 inches
Collection of the artist

15 **Portrait of Georgia O'Keeffe with Dogs** 1977
wood, pencil, oil, 52 1/2 × 55 × 60 inches
Collection of the artist

16 **Portrait of de Kooning** 1980
wood, charcoal, oil, plaster, 60 × 32 × 46 ¹/₂ inches
Collection Janet and Joseph Shein

Bishop Desmond Tutu 1988
wood, stain, fluorescent light, 75 × 79 × 50 inches
Collection of the artist

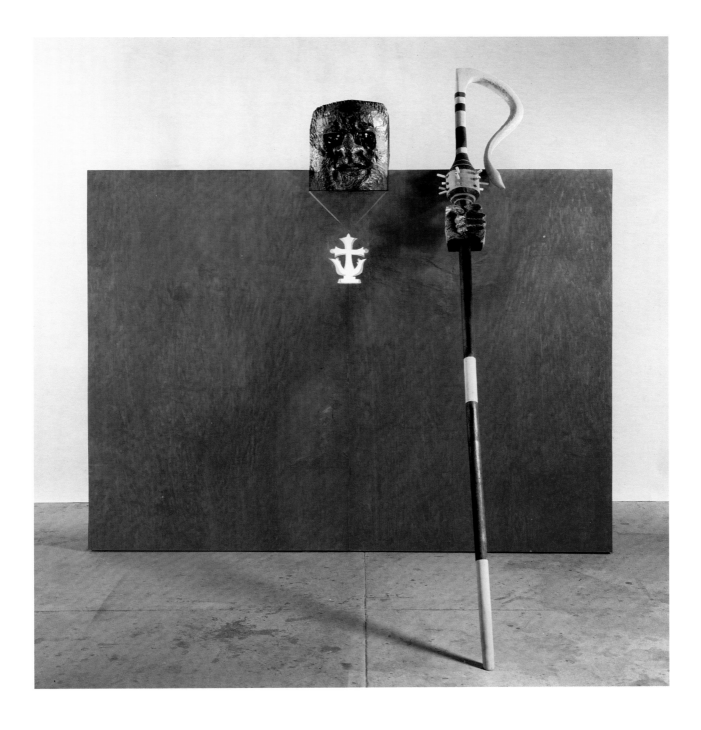

18 **Emperor Hirohito with Empress Nagako** 1989
Wood, clay, paint and fluorescent light, 76 x 71 ¹/₂ x 42 inches
Collection of the artist

wood, plaster, stain, 104 x 78 x 48 inches
Courtesy Marlborough Gallery, New York

20 **Cuban Children with Goat** 1995
wood and mixed media, 38 × 87 ³/8 × 65 inches
Courtesy Marlborough Gallery, New York

21 **Rain in the Face** 1995
wood and mixed media, 118 x 43 x 4 1/2 inches
Courtesy Marlborough Gallery, New York

22 **Tablita Dancer II** 1995
wood and mixed media, 94 × 21 3/4 × 20 inches
Courtesy Marlborough Gallery, New York

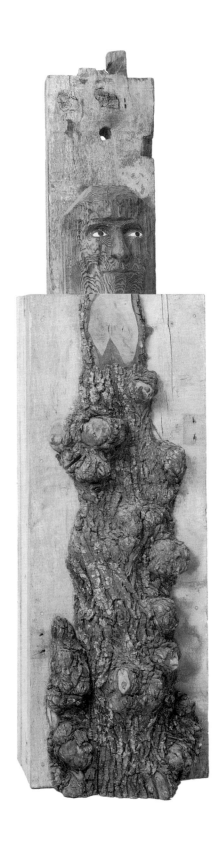

23 **Wolf Robe** 1996
wood, oil, charcoal, 90 × 33 1/2 × 13 inches
Collection of the artist

24 **General Bronze** 1997
bronze, edition of three, 102 × 109 × 55 inches
Courtesy Marlborough Gallery, New York

25 **Magritte I** 1998
wood, oil paint, plaster, charcoal, cloth, 70 x 36 x 36 inches
Collection of the artist

26 **Magritte III in Heaven** 1998
wood, oil paint, plaster, charcoal, cloth, 72 × 36 × 36 inches
Courtesy Marlborough Gallery, New York

28 **Magritte V** 1998
wood, oil paint, plaster, charcoal, cloth, 56 1/2 × 26 × 26 inches
Courtesy Marlborough Gallery, New York

wood, oil paint, plaster, charcoal, cloth, 69 × 33 × 33 inches
Collection Monica and Rick Segal

Lenders to the Exhibition

Guy and Nora Lee Barron

Albright-Knox Art Gallery, Buffalo, New York

Elizabeth B. Blake

Colorado Springs Fine Arts Center

Vera List

Marisol

Marlborough Gallery, New York

The Museum of Modern Art, New York

Roy R. Neuberger

Monica and Rick Segal

Janet and Joseph Shein

Checklist of the Exhibition

All dimensions are in inches.
Height precedes width, precedes depth.

1. *Queen*, 1957
wood and terra cotta,
29 3/4 × 13 1/2 × 9
Collection Roy R. Neuberger

2. *Figuras*, 1959
bronze, 22 1/2 × 15 1/2 × 5
Collection Blanche and Bud Blank

3. *Triumph*, 1959
bronze, 21 1/2 × 12 × 6 1/2
Collection of the artist

4. *My Wedding Cake*, 1959
bronze, 20 × 11 × 9
Collection of the artist

5. *From France*, 1960
wood construction beam, painted
and stenciled wood, carved wood,
found objects, plaster casts,
54 3/8 × 21 1/4 × 16
Collection Elizabeth B. Blake

6. *Tea for Three*, 1960
wood, acrylic paint and china,
64 × 22 × 27
Collection of the artist

7. *The Blacks*, 1962
wood, plaster, 84 × 12 × 6
Private Collection

8. *The Bathers*, 1961-62
wood and mixed media,
83 7/8 × 70 × 58
Courtesy Marlborough Gallery, NY

9. *The Family*, 1962
painted wood and mixed media
[three sections],
82 5/8 × 65 1/2 × 15 1/2
Collection of The Museum of
Modern Art; New York, New York
Advisory Committee Fund, 1962

10. *Baby Boy*, 1962-63
painted wood and mixed media,
88 × 33 × 23
Collection Vera List

11. *Baby Girl*, 1963
wood and mixed media, 74 × 35 × 47
Collection Albright-Knox Art Gallery;
Buffalo, New York
Gift of Seymour H. Knox, 1964

12. *John Wayne*, 1963
wood, pencil, oil, paint, plaster, steel,
104 × 96 × 15 [113 high installed]
Collection Colorado Springs Fine
Arts Center; Julianne Kemper Gilliam
Purchase Fund and Debutante Ball
Purchase Fund

13. *Mi Mama Y Yo*, 1968
steel and aluminum, 73 × 56 × 56
Collection of the artist
(withdrawn from the exhibition)

14. *Fishman*, 1973
wood and plaster, 50 × 22 × 30
Collection of the artist

15. *Portrait of Georgia O'Keeffe with
Dogs*, 1977
wood, pencil, oil, 52 1/2 × 55 × 60
Collection of the artist

16. *Portrait of de Kooning*, 1980
wood, charcoal, oil, plaster,
60 × 32 × 46 1/2
Collection Janet and Joseph Shein

17. *Bishop Desmond Tutu*, 1988
wood, stain, fluorescent light,
75 × 79 × 50
Collection of the artist

18. *Emperor Hirohito with Empress
Nagako*, 1989
wood, clay, paint and fluorescent light,
76 × 71 1/2 × 42
Collection of the artist

19. *John, Washington and Emily
Roebling Crossing the Brooklyn Bridge
for the First Time*, 1989
wood, plaster, stain, 104 × 78 × 48
Courtesy Marlborough Gallery, NY

20. *Cuban Children with Goat*, 1995
wood and mixed media,
38 × 87 3/8 × 65
Courtesy Marlborough Gallery, NY

21. *Rain in the Face*, 1995
wood and mixed media,
118 × 43 × 4 1/2
Courtesy Marlborough Gallery, NY

22. *Tablita Dancer II*, 1995
wood and mixed media,
94 × 21 3/4 × 20
Courtesy Marlborough Gallery, NY

23. *Wolf Robe*, 1996
wood, oil, charcoal, 90 × 33 1/2 × 13
Collection of the artist

24. *General Bronze*, 1997
bronze, unknown edition of
three, 102 × 109 × 55
Courtesy Marlborough Gallery, NY

25. *Magritte I*, 1998
wood, oil paint, plaster, charcoal,
cloth, 70 × 36 × 36
Collection of the artist

26. *Magritte III in Heaven*, 1998
wood, oil paint, plaster, charcoal,
cloth, 72 × 36 × 36
Courtesy Marlborough Gallery, NY

27. *Magritte IV*, 1998
wood, oil paint, plaster, charcoal,
cloth, 70 × 41 × 36
Collection Guy and Nora Lee Barron

28. *Magritte V*, 1998
wood, oil paint, plaster, charcoal,
cloth, 56 1/2 × 26 × 26
Courtesy Marlborough Gallery, NY

29. *Magritte VI*, 1998
wood, oil paint, plaster, charcoal,
cloth, 69 × 33 × 33
Collection Monica and Rick Segal

Marisol with brother at Foxwood, c. 1940-41

Escobar family, Switzerland c. 1933

Marisol with father, Florence, Italy c. 1933-1934

Chronology

1930
Born in Paris to Venezuelan parents, Gustavo and Josephina Escobar

c.1940-41
Attends Foxwood School, New York

1941
Attends grammar school in Venezuela

c.1946-48
Attends Westlake School for Girls, Los Angeles, CA

1946
Studies art in the evening at the Jepson School, Los Angeles, CA

c.1948
Studies with Rico Le Brun at Otis Art Institute, CA
Attends Chouinard Art School, CA

1949
Attends École des Beaux Arts, Paris, France

1950
Moves to New York
Attends The Art Students League, New York, NY, where she studies with Yasuo Kuniyoshi

1951-54
Attends The New School for Social Research, New York, NY
Studies with Hans Hofmann, New York, NY
Is influenced by Pre-Columbian art and begins working in clay

1957
Travels to Rome
Begins drawing on wood, which later evolves into her personal sculptural style
Solo exhibition Leo Castelli Gallery, New York, NY

1958
Establishes family figures as her subjects in initial wood sculptures and returns to this subject throughout her career
Participates in group exhibition *Festival of Two Worlds*, Spoleto, Italy

1959
Participates in group exhibition *The 1959 Pittsburgh International*, Carnegie Museum of Art, Pittsburgh, PA
Participates in group exhibition *Pan American Art*, The Art Institute of Chicago, IL
Participates in group exhibition *Work in 3 Dimensions*, Leo Castelli Gallery, New York, NY

1961
Introduces her self-portrait in varying techniques that becomes a trademark style in her work
Participates in group exhibition *The Art of Assemblage*, The Museum of Modern Art, New York, NY; traveled to the Museum of Modern Contemporary Art, Dallas, TX; San Francisco Museum of Modern Art, CA

1962
Incorporates a sense of self, in relation to society and family, in her work
Participates in group exhibition *Annual Exhibition of Sculpture and Drawings*, Whitney Museum of American Art, New York, NY
Participates in group exhibition *Recent Acquisitions*, The Museum of Modern Art, New York, NY
Solo exhibition Stable Gallery, New York, NY

1963

Participates in group exhibition *66th American Annual*, The Art Institute of Chicago, IL

Participates in group exhibition *Americans 1963*, The Museum of Modern Art, New York, NY

Participates in group exhibition *Mixed Media and Pop Art*, Albright-Knox Art Gallery, Buffalo, NY

1964

Works at Universal Limited Art Editions (ULAE) where she completed 5 lithographs, which juxtaposed tracings of her hands and feet with women's accessories

Participates in group exhibition *3 Generations*, Sidney Janis Gallery, New York, NY

Participates in group exhibition *Annual Exhibition*, Whitney Museum of American Art, New York, NY

Participates in group exhibition *Between the Fairs*, Whitney Museum of American Art, New York, NY

Participates in group exhibition *Boxes*, Dwan Gallery, Los Angeles, CA

Participates in group exhibition *New Realism*, Municipal Museum, The Hague, The Netherlands

Participates in group exhibition *Painting and Sculpture of a Decade*, Tate Gallery, London, England; traveled to Institute of Contemporary Art, University of Pennsylvania, Philadelphia

Participates in group exhibition *The 1964 Pittsburgh International*, Carnegie Museum of Art, Pittsburgh, PA; traveled to Washington Gallery of Modern Art, DC

Solo exhibition Stable Gallery, New York, NY

1965

Participates in group exhibition *The New American Realism*, Worcester Art Museum, MA

Participates in group exhibition *Op and Pop*, Sidney Janis Gallery, New York, NY

Solo exhibition The Arts Club of Chicago, IL

1966

Participates in group exhibition *68th American Exhibition*, The Art Institute of Chicago, IL

Participates in group exhibition *Art of the United States: 1670-1964*, Whitney Museum of American Art, New York, NY

Participates in group exhibition *Erotic Art '66*, Sidney Janis Gallery, New York, NY

Participates in group exhibition *The Harry N. Abrams Family Collection*, The Jewish Museum, New York, NY

Participates in group exhibition *Latin American Art Since Independence*, traveling exhibition sponsored by The Museum of Modern Art, New York, NY

Participates in group exhibition *New Art in Philadelphia*, Institute of Contemporary Art, University of Pennsylvania, Philadelphia

Participates in group exhibition *Tribute to Frank O'Hara*, The Museum of Modern Art, New York, NY

Participates in group exhibition *Whitney Annual: Sculpture and Prints*, Whitney Museum of American Art, New York, NY

Solo exhibition Sidney Janis Gallery, New York, NY

1967

Ventures into the sphere of public sculpture with controversial bronze, *Father Damien,* which, representing Hawaii, is installed a year later in the National Statuary Hall in the United States Capitol, Washington, DC

Participates in group exhibition *The 1967 Pittsburgh International*, Carnegie Museum of Art, Pittsburgh, PA

Participates in group exhibition *American Sculpture of the 60's*, The Los Angeles County Museum of Art, CA; traveled to the Philadelphia Museum of Art, PA

Participates in group exhibition *Homage to Marilyn Monroe*, Sidney Janis Gallery, New York, NY (catalogue)

Participates in group exhibition New York State Fair, NY

Participates in group exhibition Riverside Art Museum, CA

Participates in outdoor group exhibition *Sculptures in Environment*, New York, NY

Solo exhibition *Figures of State*, Hanover Gallery, London, England (catalogue)

Solo exhibition *Figures of State*, Sidney Janis Gallery, New York, NY (catalogue)

Marisol (center/rear) with fellow artists (clockwise, beginning lower left center): Rubin Gorswitz, Larry Rivers, Joe Baer, unidentified, John Chamberlain, Wolf Kahn, Mike Balog, Emily Mason, Robert Rauschenberg, Cy Twombly, Joseph Kosuth, Marisol, Malcolm Morley, Klaus Oldenberg, Clem Clarke, Robert Indiana, Richard Serra, Andy Warhol, and James Rosenquist, 1960s

Marisol (center), Bill Katz (left), Robert Indiana (right), 1960s

Marisol in her Broadway studio, c. 1960s

Marisol (left), Tatyana Grosman (second from left) Larry Rivers (right) at ULAE, c. 1964

1968

Travels to Asia

Participates in group exhibition *American Drawings 1968*, The Goldie Paley Gallery at Moore College of Art and Design, Philadelphia, PA

Participates in group exhibition *Art of Ancient and Modern Latin America*, Delgado Museum of Art, New Orleans, LA

Participates in group exhibition *Documenta IV*, Kassel, Germany

Participates in group exhibition *Dominant Woman Exhibition*, Finch College, New York, NY

Participates in group exhibition *The Obsessive Image*, Institute of Contemporary Art, London, England

Participates in group exhibition *The Sidney and Harriet Janis Collection*, The Museum of Modern Art, New York, NY

Participates in group exhibition *Word and Image*, The Museum of Modern Art, NY

Solo exhibition representing Venezuela *XXXIV Biennale di Venezia*, Venice, Italy

Solo exhibition Boymans Van Bueningen Museum, Rotterdam

1969

Travels for one year to the Caribbean, South America, India and the Far East and spends four months in Tahiti

Participates in group exhibition *The 1st International Exhibition of Modern Sculpture*, The Hakone Open Air Museum, Japan

Participates in group exhibition *7 Artists*, Sidney Janis Gallery, New York, NY (catalogue)

Participates in group exhibition *29th Annual Exhibition*, The Art Institute of Chicago, IL

Participates in group exhibition *American Drawings of the 60's: A Selection*, The New School, New York, NY

Participates in group exhibition *Ars'69 - Helsinki*, The Art Gallery of Ateneum, Finland

Participates in group exhibition *Contemporary American Drawing*, Fort Worth Center Museum, TX

Participates in group exhibition *Modern International Sculptures*, Hakone Open Air Museum, Japan (first prize)

Participates in group exhibition *Project 207: Recent American Drawings*, Robert Hull Fleming Museum, University of Vermont, Burlington

Participates in group exhibition *Pop Art Redefined*, Hayward Gallery, London, England

Receives Honorary Doctorate in Arts, Moore College of Art, Philadelphia, PA

1970

Creates public monument, *Bolívar and his Teacher*, glass and bronze, 12 ft., for scientific research center IVIC, Caracas, Venezuela

Returns to ULAE 1970-1973 to produce series of lithographic prints including images related to her travels to Asia, Micronesia and Polynesia, and life-size body print self portrait

Designs theater set for Luis Falco's dance "Caviar"

Begins a series of *Fish* sculptures inspired by her experience while scuba diving in Tahiti

Participates in group exhibition *7 Artists*, Sidney Janis Gallery, New York, NY

Participates in group exhibition *Carnegie International Exhibition of Painting and Sculpture*, Carnegie Museum of Art, Pittsburgh, PA

Participates in group exhibition *Contemporary Women Artists*, The Schick Art Gallery, Skidmore College, Saratoga Springs, NY; traveled to the National Arts Club, New York, NY

Participates in group exhibition *The Drawing Society's New York Regional Drawing Exhibition*, Cooper-Hewitt National Design Museum, Smithsonian Institution, New York, NY

Participates in group exhibition *L'Art Vivant American*, Foundation Maeght, Saint-Paul, France

Solo exhibition The Goldie Paley Gallery at Moore College of Art and Design, Philadelphia, PA

1971

The *2nd International Exhibition of Modern Sculpture*, The Hakone Open Air Museum, Japan (First Prize)

Participates in group exhibition *Abstract Expressionism and Pop Art*, Sidney Janis Gallery, New York, NY

Participates in group exhibition *Art Around the Automobile*, Hofstra Museum, Hofstra University, Hempstead, NY; traveled to the Institute of Contemporary Art, University of Pennsylvania, Philadelphia; Rice University Art Gallery, Houston, TX

Participates in group exhibition *Modern International Sculpture*, Hakone Open Air Museum, Japan

Solo exhibition Worcester Art Museum, MA

1972

Participates in group exhibition *350 years of Work by Women Artists*, North Carolina Museum of Art, Raleigh

Participates in group exhibition *Colossal Scale*, Sidney Janis Gallery, New York, NY

Participates in group exhibition *Contemporary Women Artists*, Roland Gibson Gallery, State University of New York at Potsdam

Participates in group exhibition *International Art Fair '72*, Basel, Switzerland

1973

Participates in group exhibition *Basel International Art Fair 4*, Sidney Janis Gallery, Basel, Switzerland

Participates in group exhibition *Drawing Exhibition*, Baltimore Museum of Art, MD

Participates in group exhibition *Jewelry as Sculpture as Jewelry*, The Institute of Contemporary Art, Boston, MA

Participates in group exhibition *Sculptor's Drawings*, Margo Leavin Gallery, Los Angeles, CA

Participates in group exhibition *Selected Editions*, Sidney Janis Gallery, New York, NY

Solo exhibition *Marisol Prints: 1961-1973*, New York Cultural Center, NY

Solo exhibition Sidney Janis Gallery, New York, NY

1974

Creates public monument, *José Gregorio Hernandez*, bronze, 12 ft., for hospital, Caracas, Venezuela

Designs theater set for Luis Falco's dance *Tiger Rag*

Participates in group exhibition *Sculpture in the Park*, North Jersey Cultural Council

Participates in group exhibition *Twenty-fifth Anniversary Part II*, Sidney Janis Gallery, New York, NY

Solo exhibition Kennedy Museum of Art, Ohio University, Athens; traveled to Columbus Museum of Art, OH

Solo exhibition Estudio Actual, Caracas, Venezuela

1975

Creates a mask series relating to her isolated heads done in the 1960s but presented like tribal masks ornamented with relics of contemporary culture

Designs theater sets for Martha Graham's dance *The Scarlet Letter* Lincoln Center, New York, NY

Participates in group exhibition *6 Americans*, Sidney Janis Gallery, New York, NY (catalogue)

Participates in group exhibition *The Art Students League of New York 100th Anniversary*, Kennedy Galleries, New York, NY

Participates in group exhibition *The Nude in American Art*, New York Cultural Center; traveled to The Minneapolis Institute of Arts, Minnesota; Blaffer Gallery, The Art Museum of the University of Houston, TX

Participates in group exhibition *Realism and Reality*, Kunsthalle Darmstadt, Darmstadt, Germany

Participates in group exhibition *Vistas Contemporaneas Latino-Americanas*, New Jersey State Council of the Arts, Trenton, NJ

Solo exhibition Makler Gallery, Philadelphia, PA

Solo exhibition Sidney Janis Gallery, New York, NY

1976

Creates public monument, *Simon Bolívar*, bronze, 6 ft. diameter, United Nations, New York, NY

Participates in group exhibition *Bologna Arte Fiera '76*, Bologna, Italy

Participates in group exhibition *Dada/Surrealist Heritage*, Sterling and Francine Clark Art Institute, Williamstown, MA

Participates in group exhibition *The Golden Door: Artist-Immigrants of America, 1876-1976*, Hirshhorn Museum and Sculpture Garden, Smithsonian Institution, Washington, DC

Participates in group exhibition *Painting and Sculpture Today*, Contemporary Art Society of the Indianapolis Museum of Art, IN

Participates in group exhibition *A Special Place*, The 59th Street Gallery, St. Louis, Missouri

Participates in group exhibition *The Year of the Woman: Reprise*, The Bronx Museum of the Arts, NY

1977

Enjoys the popularity of the college lecture circuit across the United States

Participates in group exhibition, *American Sculpture: Folk & Modern*, Queens Museum of Art, Flushing Meadows, NY

Participates in group exhibition *Artist by Artist*, organized by the Museum of Modern Art Lending Service, New York, NY

Participates in group exhibition *Contemporary Women: Consciousness and Content*, The Brooklyn Museum of Art School, NY

Participates in group exhibition *Women Artists 1976: A Celebration*, Marion Koogler McNay Art Museum, San Antonio, TX

Solo exhibition Contemporary Arts Museum, Houston, TX

Willem de Kooning, Marisol and Afro in Rome, c. 1957

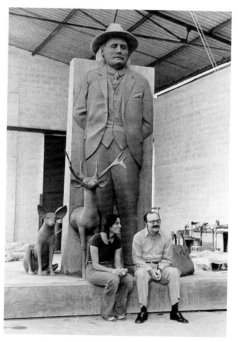

Marisol with friend Simon Consalvi, in front of monument of José Gregoria Hernandez, 1974

Marisol, c 1980

Marisol with *General Bronze*, at the Johnson Atelier foundry, Mercerville, NJ, 1997

Marisol (left) with Louise Nevelson in front of *Madonna, Child, St. Anne and St. John*, 1978, opening at Sidney Janis Gallery, 1981

Robert Indiana, Marisol, Roy Lichenstein, Tom Wesselman, Arman 1984

1978

Creates public monument, *Portrait of Padre Sojo*, bronze, 6 ft., in front of church, Caracas, Venezuela

Participates in group exhibition *7 Americans*, Sidney Janis Gallery, New York, NY

Participates in group exhibition *Another Aspect of Pop Art*, P.S. 1 Contemporary Art Center, Long Island City, NY

Participates in group exhibition *Woman: From Nostalgia to Now*, Alex Rosenberg, Fine Art, New York, NY

Receives membership into the American Academy of Arts and Letters, New York, NY (Award recipient exhibition)

Solo exhibition *Marisol Drawings*, Chatham College, Pittsburgh, PA

1979

Deigns theater set for Martha Graham's dance "Ecuatorial," Metropolitan Opera, Lincoln Center, New York, NY

Participates in group exhibition *de Kooning, Marisol, Pearlstein, Grossman, Hanson,* (curated by June Blum) Miami-Dade Community College Kendall Campus Art Gallery, Miami, FL

Participates in group exhibition *The Opposite Sex: A Realistic Viewpoint*, University of Missouri - Kansas City Gallery of Art, MO

Participates in group exhibition *Works on Paper*, Rockland Center for the Arts, West Nyack, NY

1980

Participates in group exhibition *Four From Janis*, Makler Gallery, Philadelphia, PA

Participates in group exhibition *The Language of the Symbols*, Landmark Gallery, New York, NY

1981

Designs costumes for Elisa Monte's dance *Threading*

Participates in group exhibition *Bronze*, Hamilton Gallery, New York, NY

Participates in group exhibition *International Drawing Exhibition*, The Schick Art Gallery, Skidmore College, Saratoga Springs, NY

Participates in group exhibition *New Dimensions in Drawing*, The Aldrich Museum of Contemporary Art, Ridgefield, CT

Participates in group exhibition *Romantic Drawings*, Alex Rosenberg Gallery, New York, NY

Participates in group exhibition *Sculptor's Drawings*, Max Hutchinson Gallery, New York, NY

Solo exhibition *Artists and Artistes by Marisol*, Sidney Janis Gallery, New York, NY (catalogue)

1982

Adapts the old masters through 20th century theory manipulating her media as if creating a Cubist collage (*"The Last Supper"*)

Participates in group exhibition *Flat and Figurative: 20th Century Wall Sculpture*, Zabriskie Gallery, New York, NY

Participates in group exhibition, The Aldrich Museum of Contemporary Art, Ridgefield, CT

Participates in group exhibition *Womens Art Miles Apart*, Valencia Community College, Oakland, FL

Solo exhibition Makler Gallery, Philadelphia, PA

1983

Creates public monument, *Portrait of Carlos Gardel and Three Musicians and a Dog*, bronze, 7 ft., for subway station, Caracas, Venezuela

Participates in group exhibition *American Women Artists Part I: 20th Century Pioneers*, Sidney Janis Gallery, New York, NY

Participates in group exhibition Open Air Museum of Sculpture, Middlehein, Belgium

Participates in group exhibition *Women Artists Invitational 1983: Selections from the Women Artists, Historical Archives*, Philadelphia College of Art, Philadelphia, PA

1984

Designs theater set for Elisa Monte's dance *Set in Stone*

Participates in group exhibition *Drawings since 1974*, Hirshhorn Museum & Sculpture Garden, Washington, DC

Participates in group exhibition *Masters of the Sixties*, Marisa del Re Gallery, New York, NY

Participates in group exhibition *New Portraits*, P.S. 1 Contemporary Art Center, Long Island City, NY

Participates in group exhibition *Soul Catchers*, Stellweg Seguy Gallery, New York, NY

Participates in group exhibition *Ways of Wood*, The Sculpture Center, New York, NY

Solo exhibition Sidney Janis Gallery, New York, NY

1985

Creates a public sculpture for Fiorello H. LaGuardia High School, Board of Education, New York, NY

Participates in group exhibition *American Women Artists*, Peck School, Morristown, NJ

Participates in group exhibition *Body & Soul: Figurative Sculpture*, The Contemporary Arts Center, Cincinnati, OH

Participates in group exhibition *Dorothy C. Miller, With an Eye to American Art*, Smith College Museum of Art, Northampton, MA

Participates in group exhibition *Feminists & Misogynists Together at Last*, Avenue B Gallery, New York, NY; traveled to Center on Contemporary Art, Seattle, WA

Participates in group exhibition *Forms in Wood: American Sculpture of the 1950s*, Philadelphia Museum of Art, PA

Participates in group exhibition *The Gathering of the Avant Garde: The Lower East Side 1950-1970*, Kenkeleba House, New York, NY

Participates in group exhibition *In Three Dimensions: Recent Sculpture by Women*, Pratt Manhattan Gallery, Schafler Gallery, Pratt Institute, New York, NY

Participates in group exhibition *Selection of 20th Century Portraits in Three Dimension*, Cleveland Center for Contemporary Art, OH

Participates in group exhibition *Sights for Small Eyes*, Heckscher Museum of Art, Huntington, NY

Participates in group exhibition *Wood, Water & Stone*, (curated by Corinne Robins) 909 Third Avenue, New York, NY

Receives an Award of Excellence in Design, The Arts Commission of the City of New York for a sculpture at Fiorello H. La Guardia High School, New York

1986

Participates in group exhibition *American Art: American Women*, Stamford Museum and Nature Center, Stamford, CT (traveled)

Participates in group exhibition *Drawings by Sculptors*, Nohra Haime Gallery, New York, NY

Participates in group exhibition *Pop: Then and Now*, Castle Gallery, College of New Rochelle, NY

Participates in group exhibition *Universal Images: People and Nature in Sculpture*, 909 Third Avenue and the Mendik Co., New York, NY

Receives Honorary Doctorate in Arts, Rhode Island School of Design, Providence, RI

1987

Creates public monument, *Romulo Betancourt*, bronze, 6 ft. diameter, Garden, Caracas, Venezuela

Participates in group exhibition *American Art Today: The Portrait*, The Art Museum at Florida International University, Miami

Participates in group exhibition *The Artist's Mother: Portraits and Homages*, Heckscher Museum of Art, Huntington, New York; traveled to National Portrait Gallery, Smithsonian Institution, Washington, DC

Participates in group exhibition *Monte Carlo Sculpture '87*, Marisa del Re Gallery, New York, NY

1988

Participates in group exhibition *Centennial Exhibition of the National Association of Women Artists*, Nassau County Museum of Art, Roslyn Harbor, NY

Participates in group exhibition *Just Like a Woman*, Greenville County Museum of Art, Greenville, SC

Participates in group exhibition *The New Sculpture Group: A Look Back 1957-1962*, New York Studio School of Drawing, Painting, and Sculpture Gallery, NY

Participates in group exhibition *Urban Figures*, Whitney Museum of American Art at Philip Morris, New York, NY

Participates in group exhibition *XLIII Biennale di Venezia*, Venice, Italy

Solo exhibition Boca Raton Museum of Art, FL

Solo exhibition Dolly Fiterman Gallery, Minneapolis, MN

1989

Participates in group exhibition *100 Drawings by Women*, Hillwood Art Gallery, Long Island University, Brookville, NY; traveled to BlumHelman Gallery, New York, NY; Clara M. Eagle Gallery, Murray State University, Murray, KY; Grand Rapids Art Museum, MI; University Art Gallery, University of North Texas, Denton; Richard F. Brush Gallery, St. Lawrence University, Canton, NY; The University of Oklahoma Museum of Art, Norman; Albany Museum of Art, GA; traveled internationally to Caracas, Venezuela; Rio de Janeiro, Brazil; Montevideo, Paraguay; Mexico City, Mexico

Participates in group exhibition *Body Fragments*, Shea & Baker, New York, NY

Participates in group exhibition *Positive I.D.*, The Southern Alleghenies Museum of Art, Loretto, PA

Solo exhibition *Marisol: Recent Sculpture*, Galerie Tokoro, Tokyo, Japan

Solo exhibition Sidney Janis Gallery, New York, NY

1990

Participates in group exhibition *The 80's: A Post Pop Generation*, The Southern Alleghenies Museum of Art, Loretto, PA

Participates in group exhibition *Body Language: The Figure in the Art of Our Time*, Rose Art Museum, Brandeis University, Waltham, MA

Participates in group exhibition *Seoul International Art Festival*, The National Museum of Contemporary Art, Korea

1991

Creates a public monument for the American Merchant Marine Memorial, Promenade Battery Park, Pier A, Port of New York

Participates in group exhibition *Masterworks of Contemporary Sculpture, Painting and Drawing: The 1930's to the 1990's*, Bellas Artes, Sante Fe, New Mexico

Participates in group exhibition *Show of Strength (in support of MADRE)*, Anne Plumb Gallery, New York, NY

Solo exhibition *Marisol Portrait Sculpture*, National Portrait Gallery, Smithsonian Institution, Washington, DC (catalogue)

Solo exhibition *Marisol: Selected Sculpture*, Riva Yares Gallery, Scottsdale, AZ

1992

Designs theater set for Martha Graham's dance, *The Eyes of the Goddess*, Lincoln Center, New York, NY

Participates in group exhibition *20th Century Masters: Works on Paper*, Sidney Janis Gallery, New York, NY

Participates in group exhibition *Figures of Contemporary Sculpture (1970-1990): Images of Man*, Isetan Museum, Tokyo, Japan; traveled to Daimaru Museum, Osaka; Hiroshima City Museum of Contemporary Art, Hiroshima

Receives an Honorary Doctorate in Fine Arts, State University of New York at Buffalo

Receives The 11th Annual Art Commission Awards for Excellence in Design, The Art Commission of the City of New York, for the American Merchant Mariner's Memorial, New York

Solo exhibition *Images of Japan*, Tenri Cultural Institute, New York, NY

Solo exhibition *Marisol*, New Jersey Center for Visual Arts, Summit, NJ (catalogue)

1993

Creates a series of Native Americans as sculptural subjects during the 1990s

Participates in group exhibition *Figure: Contemporary Sculpture*, Marlborough Gallery, New York, NY

Participates in group exhibition *Lateinamerikanische Kunst im 20, Jahrhundert*, Museum Ludwig and Josef-Haubrich-Kunsthalle, Cologne, Germany

Participates in group exhibition *The League at the Cape*, Provincetown Art Association and Museum, Provincetown, MA

Participates in group exhibition *Venezuelan Masters of the 20th Century in American Collections*, The Venezuelan Center Gallery, New York, NY

1995

Participates in group exhibition *Artist's Choice: Elizabeth Murray*, The Museum of Modern Art, New York, NY

Receives Medal of Honor, National Arts Club, New York, NY

Solo retrospective exhibition *Marisol*, The Hakone Open Air Museum; traveled to The Museum of Modern Art, Shiga, Iwai City Art Museum, Fukushima, Kagoshima City Museum of Art, (catalogue)

Solo exhibition *Recent Works*, Marlborough Gallery, New York, NY (catalogue)

1996

Participates in group exhibition *Latin Viewpoints: into the Mainstream*, Nassau County Museum of Art, Roslyn Harbor, NY

1997

Participates in group exhibition *ART 1997 CHICAGO: 5th Annual Expo of International Galleries Featuring Modern and Contemporary Art*, Navy Pier, Chicago, IL

Participates in group exhibition *The Feminine Image*, Nassau County Museum of Art, Roslyn Harbor, NY (catalogue)

Participates in group exhibition *Spring 1997 Exhibition: Marisol, Robert Murray, Jay Wholley*, Grounds for Sculpture, Hamilton, NJ

Receives Gabriela Mistral Inter-American Prize for Culture, sponsored by La Organización de los Estados Americanos (OEA), for cultural enrichment in the field of Science and Plastic Arts

Solo exhibition Grounds for Sculpture, Hamilton, NJ (catalogue)

1998

Participates in group exhibition *Stages of Creation: Public Sculpture by National Academicians*, National Academy of Design Museum and School of Fine Arts, New York, NY

Participates in group exhibition *Coming Off the Wall*, The Susquehanna Art Museum, Harrisburg, PA

Solo exhibition Marlborough Gallery, New York, NY (catalogue)

1999

Participates in group exhibition *IXth Show of Latin American Painting and Sculpture*, Galería Espacio, San Salvador, El Salvador

1999-2000

Solo exhibition Art Museum of the Americas, Organization of American States, Washington, DC

2000

Participates in group exhibition *Doce Artistas del XX*, Espacios Unión, Caracas, Venezuela

2001

Solo exhibition Marlborough Gallery, New York, NY

Solo exhibition Neuberger Museum of Art, Purchase College, State University of New York, Purchase, NY

Public Collections

Albright-Knox Art Gallery, Buffalo, NY

The Art Institute of Chicago, IL

The Arts Club of Chicago, IL

Memphis Brooks Museum of Art, Memphis, TN

The Corcoran Gallery of Art, Washington, DC

Galería de Arte Nacional, Caracas, Venezuela

The Hakone Open Air Museum, Japan

Hirshhorn Museum and Sculpture Garden, Smithsonian Institution, Washington, DC

John and Mable Ringling Museum of Art, Sarasota, FL

The Metropolitan Museum of Art, New York, NY

The Minneapolis Institute of Arts, MN

Museum of Contemporary Art, Chicago, IL

El Museo de Arte Contemporáneo Caracas, Venezuela

Museum of Contemporary Art, Chicago, IL

The Museum of Modern Art, New York, NY

The Wallraf-Richartz Museum, Cologne, Germany

The Tokushima Modern Art Museum, Japan

Whitney Museum of American Art, New York, NY

Yale University Art Gallery, New Haven, CT

Selected Bibliography

Periodicals and Newspapers

"Americans 1963." *Art International* (June 25, 1963): 71

Amman, J.C. "Venedig: 34 Biennale." *Werk* (August 1968): 566

Andre, Michael. "Marisol at Marlborough." *Art in America* (December 1995): 91-92

_____. "New York Reviews: Marisol." *ARTnews* (May 1975): 94

_____. "Reviews and Previews: Marisol." *ARTnews* (December 1973): 90

Angeline, John. "Marisol." *Art Nexus* (January/March 1996): 124-125

Antin, David. "Portrait." *Kunstwerk* (April-June 1966): 29

Ashton, Dore. "Exhibition at Stable." *Studio International* (May 1964): 213-214

_____. "New York Commentary: Historicism & Respect for Tradition." *Studio International* (June, 1966): 278

"Art Collectors-A Life Involvement." *Time* (March 29, 1968): 68

"Art for Everyday Living: Painted Furs." *Art in America* (October 1963): 97

"Art: Eros in Polyester." *Newsweek* (October 10, 1966): 102-103

"Art: How to Portray a Martyr." *Time* (1967): 83

"Art: Marisol." *Time* (June 7, 1963): 76-79

"Art: Sculpture-The Dollmaker." *Time* (May 28, 1965): 80-81

"Artist in Focus: Marisol." *American Artist* (August 1986): 74

Barnitz, Jacqueline. "The Marisol Mask." *Artes Hispanicas* (Autumn 1967): 35

Baro, Gene. "Gathering of Americans." *Arts Magazine* (September 1963): 28

Barrio-Garay, J.L. "El auge de la escultura en exposiciones individuales." *Goya* (July-August 1973): 41

Barry, Edward. "The Art of Marisol: Intriguing Objects Fashioned on Wood." *Chicago Tribune* (December 22, 1965): sec. 2: 9

Benedict, Michael. "New York Letter." *Art International* (October 1966): 53

Benko, Susana. "Del Siglo que se va. Doce Artistas del XX." *Art Nexus* (March 2000): 118-119

Berman, Avis. "A Bold and Incisive Way of Portraying Movers and Shakers." *Smithsonian* (February 1984): 54-63

Bernstein, Roberta. "Marisol as Portraitist: Artist & Artistes." *Arts Magazine* (May 1981): 112

_____. "Marisol's Self Portraits: The Dream and the Dreamer." *Arts Magazine* (March 1985): 86-89

Boime, Albert. "The Postwar Redefinition of Self: Marisol's Yearbook Illustrations for the Class of '49." *American Art* (Spring 1996): 91-93

Brown, Gordon. "Marisol at Janis." *Arts Magazine* (June 1966): 45

Brozan, Nadine. "Chronicle." *The New York Times* (January 11, 1995): sec. B: 6

Burchard, Hank. "Marisol's Sunny, Sly Portraits." *The Washington Post/Weekend* (April 5, 1991): 59

Butler, J.T. "Worcester Art Museum Exhibition." *Connoisseur* (January 1972): 59

Campbell, Lawrence. "Marisol." *ARTnews* (November 1967): 60

_____. "Marisol at Janis." *ARTnews* (Summer 1966): 13

Campos, Manuel. "Mesa de Discusion: Marisol Triunfa en Nueva New York." *La Revista* (Caracas) (June 14, 1964): 5

Canaday, John. "Americans Once More." *The New York Times* (May 26, 1963): sec. 2:11

_____. "Art: 15 Exhibit at the Modern." *The New York Times* (May 22, 1963): 38

_____. "Life Size Dolls on Display at Janis." *The New York Times* (April 16, 1966): 29

_____. "Toys by Artists are Good Art and Good Toys." *The New York Times* (December 22, 1963): sec. 2:14

Carroll, Karen. "Marisol." *School Arts* (November 1986): 23

Coates, Robert M. "The Art Galleries: Extremes." *The New Yorker* (December 11, 1965): 222

"Collectors: From Mondrian to Martial Airs." *Time* (January 26, 1968): 56

Cooper, James F. "Trashing of Old Masters is Latest Outrage in Liberal Art." *New York Herald Tribune* (June 1984): sec. B: 1

De Lamater, Peg. "Marisol's Public and Private de Gaulle." *American Art* (Spring 1996): 91-93

Derfner, Phyllis. "New York: Marisol." *Art International* (May 15, 1975): 67

Dreishpoon, Douglas. "Marisol Portrait Sculpture." (Review) *Art Journal* (Winter 1991): 94

Edelman, Robert G. "Marisol." *Art in America* (October 1984): 189

Edinberg, Joyce. "Sculptor Marisol Re-creates 'Last Supper' in Wood, Stone." *The Daily Journal* (June 30, 1984): 16

Feldman, B.W. "Portrait Gallery Displays Marisol's Clever Sculptures." *The Capital* (Annapolis, Maryland) (Wednesday, April 17, 1991): sec. B: 10

"Fifty-six Painters and Sculptors." *Art in America* (August 1964): 77

Gardner, Paul. "Who is Marisol?" *ARTnews* (May 1988): 146

Genauer, Emily. "57th Street and Environs: Marisol." *The New York Herald Tribune* (April 16, 1966): 7

_____. "On Art: Happy Hunting in a Cornucopia." *The New York Herald Tribune* (November 25, 1967): 6

Gibson, Eric. "Marisol." *ARTnews* (December 1995):138

Glueck, Grace. "A Marisol Sculpture Creates a Storm, and Loses, in Hawaii." *The New York Times* (March 31, 1967): 29

_____. "It's Not Pop, It's Not Op - It's Marisol." *The New York Times* Magazine (March 7, 1965): 34

_____. "Marisol Shows Her Brooklyn Bridge Memorial." *The New York Times* (April 16, 1988): 11

Gold, Barbara. "Portrait of Marisol." *Interplay* (January 1968): 52

Goldberg, Jeff. "Marisol—In Her Own Words." *People Magazine* (March 24, 1975): 40

Gonzalez, Miguel. "Ninth Show of Latin American Painting and Sculpture." *Art Nexus* (February-April 1999): 102-103

Gosling, Nigel. "Gallery Guide." *The Observer* (September 24 1967): 24

Gray, Cleve. "Tatyana Grosman's Workshop." *Art in America* (December-January 1966): 85

Grove, Nancy. "Forum: Marisol's Black Bird Love." *Drawing* (September-October 1993): 58

Heartney, Eleanor. "Report From Seoul. Korea Opens the Door." *Art in America* (April 1991): 67

Heinemann, Susan. "Reviews: Marisol." *Artforum* 13,9 (May 1975): 77

Henry, Gerrit. "Reviews and Previews: Marisol." *ARTnews* (Summer 1973): 92

Hess, Thomas B. "The Disrespectful Hand Maiden." *ARTnews* (January 1965): 38

_____. "The Phony Crisis in American Art." *ARTnews* (Summer 1963): 24

Horowitz, Leonard. "What's Wrong With Wrong?" *The Village Voice* (March 12, 1964): 8

Janis, Sidney. "Marisol." *Arts Magazine* (November 1984): 38

"John Wayne, Who Rides Off Artfully in All Directions." *Life* (December 20, 1963): 102

Kimmelman, Michael. "Marisol." *The New York Times* (May 19, 1988): 33

Kingsley, April. "New York Letter: Marisol." *Art International* (October 1973): 53

Kiplinger, Suzanne. "Art: Marisol at Stable." *The Village Voice* (November 20, 1962): 10

Kisselgoff, April. "Graham's Legacy: Consistent Change." *The New York Times/Arts & Leisure* (October 27,1991): sec. 2: 7

Kozloff, Max. " New York Letter: Marisol." *Art International* (September 1962): 35

Kuh, Katherine. "The Fine Arts: Notes of a Peripatetic Gallerygoer." *Saturday Review* (April 25, 1964): 71

Larson, Kay. "Supper with Marisol." *New York Magazine* (June 4, 1984): 70

Leimbach, Dulcie. "The American Merchant Mariners Memorial." (Review) *The New York Times* (January 3 1992): sec. C: 23

Lewis, JoAnn. "Marisol's Heady People." *The Washington Post* (Friday, April 5, 1991): B1-B2

Loring, John. "Marisol's Diptych: Impressions, Tracings, Hatchings." *Arts Magazine* (April 1973): 69

_____. "Marisol Draws." *Arts Magazine* (March 1975): 66

Lund, Kay. "Statue Urged to Being Anew of Selection of Damien Statue." *Honolulu Star Bulletin* (May 8, 1967): 99

Marchiori, G. " La Biennale De Venise enlisee dans la leggier." (December 1964): 134

"Marisol...a Brilliant Sculptress Shapes the Heads of State." *Look* (November 14, 1967): 78

Mastai, M.L. D'Otrange. "Marisol: Stable Gallery." *The Arts Review* (July 14, 1962): 28

_____." New York News." *The Arts Review* (July 14, 1962): 23

Mayer, Phil. "Public Divided on Damien Model." *Honolulu Star Bulletin* (May 8, 1967): 99

Mellow, James R. "New York." *Art International* (November 1967): 59

_____. "New York Letter." *Art International* (January 1968): 64

Metken, G. "Dokumenta." *Deutsche Bauzeitung* (October 1968): 795

Neu, Renee S. "The Artist as Jeweler." *Art in America* (November-December 1967): 76

"New York: exposition des sculptures dans Central Park." (photo), *Architecture d'Aujourd'hui* (December 1967): 55

O'Doherty, Brian. "Marisol: The Enigma of the Self-Image." *The New York Times* (March 1,1964): sec. 2: 23

Perrault, John. "The Identity Behind Marisol's Face." *The Village Voice* (May 17,1973): 46

Petersen, Valerie. "Exhibition at Stable Gallery." *ARTnews* (May1962): 10

_____."Reviews and Previews: Marisol." *ARTnews* (April 1961): 10

Phillips, Deborah C. "New York Reviews: Marisol." *ARTnews* (September 1981): 231

Pierce, Nan. "New York Gallery Notes." *Art in America* (March-April 1966): 128

Raynor, Vivien. "Art: Marisol Sculpture from Leonardo Painting." *The New York Times* (June 1, 1984): sec. 2:23

_____. "Exhibition at Stable." *Arts Magazine* (September 1962): 44

Roberts, C. " Lettre de New York." *Aujourd'hui* (May 1963): 48

Rosenberg, Harold. "From Pollock to Pop: Twenty Years of Painting and Sculpture." *Holiday* (March 1966): 96

Ross, Felice. "Marisol." *Pictures on Exhibit 3* (December 1967): 17

Rykwert, Joseph. "54-64 mostra a London." *Domus* (October 1964): 54

_____. "Reviews and Previews: New York Painters' and Sculptors' Drawings." *ARTnews* (January 1958): 19

Schwartz, Barbara. "Sidney Janis Exhibition." *Craft Horizons* (August 1975): 44

_____. "Sidney Janis Gallery Exhibition." *Craft Horizons* (August 1973): 29

Schwendenwien, Jude. "Marisol: (Marlborough Gallery, NY: exhibition)." *Sculpture* (January 1996): 77

Shepley, James R. Cover & Letter from Publisher *Time* (March 3, 1967): 4

Sheppard, Eugenia. "Inside Fashion: She Likes Portraits." *The New York Herald Tribune* (April 19, 1966): 21

Siegel, Jeanne. "Marisol." *Pictures on Exhibit* (January 1966): 12

Silverthorne, Jeanne. "Marisol." *Artforum* (October 1984): 90

Simon, Herbert. "Marisol, Robert Murray and Jay Wholley." *Sculpture* (September 1997): 73-74

Simon, Joan. "Chers Maitres." *Art in America* (October 1981): 120-121

Slesin, Suzanne. "The New York Artist in Residence." *ARTnews* (November 1978): 74

Stein, Harvey. "Artists in Focus: Marisol." *American Artist* (August 1986): 74

Steinem, Gloria. "Marisol: The Face Behind the Mask." *Glamour* (June 1964): 92

Sweeny, Jim. "Marisol's Satirical Carvings." *The Fairfax Journal* (Virginia) (Friday, July 5, 1991): B4.

Sydhoff, Beate. "Marisol." *Konstrevy* Haft Nr. 5/6 (1966): 230

"The New Whitney." *Newsweek* (October 3, 1966): 101

"The Third Dimension." *Newsweek* (May 8, 1967): 99

Tillim, Sidney. "In the Galleries: Marisol." *Arts Magazine* (April 1964): 28

Tyler, Parker. "Reviews and Previews: Marisol." *ARTnews* (November 1957): 14

Vergani, Leonardo. "Una Scultrici Transforma I Personaggi in Sarcofaghi." *Corriere Della Sera* (September 22, 1967): 3

Wasserman, Edith. "Remember Dada? Today We Can Call Him Pop." *Art Education* (May 1966): 12

Westfall, Stephen. "Arts Review: Marisol." *Arts Magazine* (June, 1981): 25

_____. "Art Reviews: Marisol." *Arts Magazine* (November 1984): 38

Whiting, Cecile. "Figuring Marisol's Femininities." *RACAR* (1991): 73-90.

Willard, Charlotte. "Eye to I." *Art in America* (March-April, 1966): 52

_____. "In the Art Galleries." *The New York Post* (December 12, 1965): 47

"Wood Carver's Comeback: Young U.S. Sculptors Revive Neglected Art." *Life* (July 14, 1958): 54

Yarrow, Andrew. "The Whitney Returns to Down Under." *The New York Times* (April 16, 1988): 12

"Young Talent USA." *Art in America* (June 1963): 50

Books and Catalogues

Andersen, Wayne. *American Sculpture in Process: 1930-1970.* Boston: New York Graphic Society, 1975

Ashton, Dore. *American Art Since 1945.* New York: Oxford University Press, 1982

_____. *Modern American Sculpture.* New York: Harry N. Abrams, 1968

Berkson, Bill. *In Memory of My Feelings: A Selection of Poems by Frank O'Hara.* New York: The Museum of Modern Art, No. 5, Limited Edition of 2500 copies, designed by Susan Draper Tundisi, published by Crafton Graphic Co., 1967

Bernstein, Roberta. *Marisol.* New York: Art Life Ltd., 1995

Bernstein, Roberta and Yoshiaki Tono. *Marisol.* Tokyo: Galerie Tokoro, 1989

Burnham, Jack. *Beyond Modern Sculpture.* New York: George Braziller, 1968

Calas, Nicholas and Elena. *Icons and Images of the Sixties.* New York: E.P. Dutton, 1971

Craven, Wayne. *Sculpture in America.* New York: Thomas Y. Crowell, 1968

Creeley, Robert. *Presences: A Text for Marisol.* New York: Charles Scribner's Sons, 1976

Gablik, Suzi and John Russell. *Pop Art Redefined.* London: Thames and Hudson, 1969

Grove, Nancy. *Magical Mixtures: Marisol Portrait Sculpture.* Washington, DC: Smithsonian Institution Press for the National Portrait Gallery, 1991

Katz, William, ed. *Stamps Indelibly, A Collection of Rubber Stamp Prints,* Edition of 225, New York: Multiples, Inc., 1967

Lunn, Margaret R. (Introduction) *Marisol.* New Jersey Center for the Visual Arts: Harvard Printing Company, New York, 1991

Mahsun, Carol Anne, ed. *Pop Art: the Critical Dialogue.* Ann Arbor: UMI Research Press, 1989

Marisol. Caracas: Estudio Actual, 1973

Marisol. Chicago: The Arts Club of Chicago, 1966

Marisol. Rotterdam: Museum Boymans-van Beuningen, 1968

Marisol. Worcester, Massachusetts: Worcester Art Museum, 1971

Medina, José Ramon. *Marisol.* Caracas: Ediciones Armitano, 1968

Miller, Dorothy. Ed. *Americans.* New York: The Museum of Modern Art, 1963

Mitchell, Joan. *Contemporary American Women Artists.* San Rafael: Cedco Publishing, 1991

Nemser, Cindy. *Art Talk.* New York: Charles Scribner's Sons, 1975

Pierre, José. *An Illustrated Dictionary of Pop Art.* London: Eyre Methuen, 1975

Ratcliff, Carter. *Marisol: Realms of Perceptual Memory.* New York: Marlborough Gallery, Inc., 1998

Rose, Barbara. *American Art Since 1900.* New York: Aron, 1967

Rubinstein, Charlotte Streifer. *American Women Artists.* New York: Aron, 1982

Seitz, William C. *The Art of Assemblage.* New York: The Museum of Modern Art, Doubleday and Co., Inc., 1961

Tuchman, Maurice. *American Sculpture of the Sixties.* Los Angeles: Los Angeles County Museum of Art, 1968